To: _____

From: _____

Other books by Gregory E. Lang:

Why a Daughter Needs a Dad
Why a Son Needs a Dad
Why I Love Grandma
Why I Love Grandpa
Why a Son Needs a Mom
Why a Daughter Needs a Mom
Why I Chose You
Why I Love You
Why I Need You
Why We Are a Family
Why We Are Friends
Brothers and Sisters
Thank You, Mom
Love Signs
Simple Acts
Life Maps

Thank You, Dad

· 100 Reasons Why I Am Grateful for You ·

Gregory E. Lang

Cumberland House

Nashville, Tennessee

THANK YOU, DAD
PUBLISHED BY CUMBERLAND HOUSE PUBLISHING, INC.
431 Harding Industrial Drive
Nashville, TN 37211

Copyright © 2007 by Gregory E. Lang

All rights reserved. No part of this book may be reproduced or transmitted in any form or by any means, electronic or mechanical, including photocopying and recording, or by any information storage and retrieval system, without permission in writing from the publisher, except for brief quotations in critical reviews or articles.

ISBN-13: 978-1-58182-604-3
ISBN-10: 1-58182-604-4

Cover design: JulesRulesDesign
Cover photograph: Janet Lankford-Moran
Text design: Lisa Taylor
Interior photographs: Gregory E. Lang

Printed in the United States of America
1 2 3 4 5 6 7 8 — 12 11 10 09 08 07

To Dad—thank you for everything.

Introduction

I have much to be thankful for—the love and support of my family, my health, my many friends, my material comforts, and more. When I stop to think about how my life has unfolded, I remind myself to be humble and grateful for what I have. In those quiet moments of reflection, I count my debt to my family, friends, and mentors who have given me generous help along every step of my life's journey. My greatest debt is for what my parents gave me, the solid foundation on which my life began to take shape. It is that foundation, the one my father helped build for me, which this book is about.

Now well into my midlife, I am evermore thankful for my dad, especially when, as a parent myself, I think about what is required of a father to set into place the building blocks that will support and nurture a family for a lifetime. With this book I hope I begin to take account of and adequately thank my father for doing all he could to make sure I had the opportunities I wanted, as well as those he hoped for my siblings and me. He labored hard to create those opportunities and provide for his family, sometimes even holding two jobs to make it all happen. I used to think he worked too much; now I realize he worked as much as he did so that we would never do without.

My dad complimented me one day for making time for my family, for making sure my work did not take over my life and cause me to be an absent dad. He then told me he could recall only one weekend in his childhood that his father spent in recreation with him. That was the moment I regretted that I had judged him for not being around as much as I wished he had been, because I finally realized how much time he *had* given his children in spite of the long hours he spent working to support his family.

Indeed, a father's major responsibility is to provide for his family. Sometimes when I feel stressed by my role as provider I succumb to the opinion that the difficulties of that task go unrecognized and without gratitude, but then I remember my family is only half the size of the one my dad provided for. That is when I feel most proud of him, when I remember how he pushed himself during his free time to acquire the skills necessary for a better career, how he helped us kids pursue our dreams at the expense of his own, and how he always stepped in to help if trouble of any kind befell any of us. He set an example for what I am supposed to do as a father, an example I still aspire to.

The things my dad has done for me over the years are indeed numerous, and regrettably I'm sure I can't recollect them all no matter how hard I might try. Yet I often smile when I recall how my dad kept our bicycles and go-cart in good working order, showed me how to hit a curveball and cast a lure, worked with me on a Boy Scout project to earn a coveted merit badge, and taught me how to do things for myself as we tinkered with the car or the house on weekend afternoons. He also patiently taught me to drive, and years later, as I gave my own children driving lessons, I remembered his laughter as I once drove his pickup truck into a ditch.

There are, I think, a few universal hallmarks of a good parent: unconditional love, unfailing support, endless affection, and concern. Perhaps there are also a few additional hallmarks of a good father: self-sacrifice, perseverance, and forethought. These are the characteristics that distinguish my dad in my heart and mind.

Of all the loving gestures, caring interventions, personal sacrifices, and life lessons I could thank my father for, the one thing that means the most to me, and for which I am immeasurably grateful, is that he continues to do the fatherly things he has always done for his children. My dad lives to be a good father to my siblings and me. Even though I now say thanks for the countless things my father has done for me, the embarrassing truth is I rarely showed appreciation for what he did for me when I was young. The time to remedy that youthful error has come.

And so I've written this book to say, "Thank you, Dad." With it I publicly and enthusiastically acknowledge the many sacrifices he made on my behalf, the lessons he taught me, and the time and love he gave me all those years ago. I am using these pages to tell him, "I can't possibly thank you enough for everything you did, but I'm going to try." Even then, the expressions of gratitude that follow, whether simple, silly, or profound, are only the beginning of what I want to say to my dad and what I believe other children, young and old, want and should say to theirs (and you can by writing your own personal message of thanks in the last pages of this book).

I think being not just a father but also a good dad is the greatest challenge a man can have. I am proud of how well my father stood up to that challenge, and I now recognize his sacrifices, even though as I write these words I know he will humbly say that I've given him too much credit. No, Dad, I haven't. You did it all and so much more. I love you and thank you for everything.

Thank You, Dad

Thank you, Dad, for

being the kind of parent I could look up to.

Thank you, Dad, for

encouraging me to use my imagination.

Thank you, Dad, for . . .

making sure I stayed healthy.

*making sure my toys were safe
for me to play with.*

teaching me how to swim.

Thank you, Dad, for . . .

explaining everything I needed to know

about the birds and the bees.

making sure I learned to understand and respect "no."

requiring me to respect authority

and not abuse my own.

Thank you, Dad, for

not putting up with my misbehavior.

Thank you, Dad, for

making sure I was as happy as I could be.

Thank you, Dad, for . . .

loving me so much when it didn't seem

I loved you at all.

        teaching me how to conduct myself in relationships

                with family and friends.

        setting limits on me when I needed them.

Thank you, Dad, for . . .

helping me to understand the opposite sex.

helping me understand the significance of current events.

not allowing me to smoke and use drugs.

Thank you, Dad, for

making sure I was always a good sport, win or lose.

Thank you, Dad, for . . .

making sure I learned and used good manners.

teaching me to embrace my civic and patriotic duties.

giving me all the opportunities you could.

Thank you, Dad, for

always making time to play with me
when I needed your attention.

Thank you, Dad, for . . .

caring for my pets even though I said I would do everything.

*all those times you carried me
on your shoulders.*

protecting me from the dangers I couldn't see.

Thank you, Dad, for

requiring me to do chores. It taught me responsibility.

Thank you, Dad, for

keeping a watchful eye on all of us.

Thank you, Dad, for

helping me to practice, practice, practice.

Thank you, Dad, for

teaching me how to resist peer pressure.

Thank you, Dad, for . . .

being someone I could always count on.

*forgiving me for all the stress
I'm sure I caused you.*

not tolerating my laziness and apathy.

indulging my sometimes strange selection of friends.

Thank you, Dad, for . . .

holding me close when I needed your comfort.

always coming when I called for you,
and for coming even when I didn't think I needed you.

telling me so often that you love me.

helping me find myself.

Thank you, Dad, for

reassuring me when I doubted myself.

Thank you, Dad, for

praising me when I accomplished something important to me.

Thank you, Dad, for

showing me how to make good use of idle hands.

Thank you, Dad, for

showing me the gentle side of men.

Thank you, Dad, for . . .

teaching me how and when to ask for help.

helping prepare me for supporting my own family.

teaching me how to slam dunk an interview.

expecting me to be a good and responsible employee.

Thank you, Dad, for

teaching me how to become a good spouse and parent.

Thank you, Dad, for

teaching me how to drive.

Thank you, Dad, for

taking me places to explore the wonders of the world.

Thank you, Dad, for . . .

not giving me an embarrassing nickname.

making sure I didn't act too big for my britches.

pushing me to do the things I didn't want to do,
but needed to do.

listening intently to what I was trying to say.

Thank you, Dad, for

encouraging me to try new things.

Thank you, Dad, for

making sure I got plenty of exercise.

Thank you, Dad, for

expecting my best but not pressuring me
beyond my capabilities.

Thank you, Dad, for . . .

teaching me how to negotiate fairly but assertively.

being such a great example of what I should be like when I grew up.

teaching me to give of myself more than I take from others.

always being ready to help or protect me,

no matter how old I am.

Thank you, Dad, for

letting me go when I was ready to test myself.

Thank you, Dad, for

helping me to take care of the things
I couldn't handle by myself.

Thank you, Dad, for

standing by me when times were tough for me.

Thank you, Dad, for

always showing your pride in me.

Thank you, Dad, for

showing me how to be enthusiastic
about life's simple pleasures.

Thank you, Dad, for

teaching me the importance of planning for the future.

Thank you, Dad, for . . .

answering all those "how" and "why" questions I asked.

showing me a better way when I did something wrong.

urging me to achieve what others thought was beyond my reach.

helping me to understand why I can't always have my way.

Thank you, Dad, for

attending all of my events.

Thank you, Dad, for

teaching me how to deal diplomatically
with prejudice and discrimination.

▪   ▪   ▪   ▪   ▪   ▪

Thank you, Dad, for . . .

forgiving my infractions, but holding me

accountable for them.

admitting when you were wrong;
it taught me character.

making me suffer the consequences of my ill actions;

it taught me to use good judgment.

expecting me to be gracious when others

were generous toward me.

Thank you, Dad, for

always being ready to catch me should I fall.

Thank you, Dad, for

not letting me grow up too fast.

Thank you, Dad, for
all the sacrifices you made to give me the best life you could.

Thank you, Dad, for . . .

giving me comfort when I was alone or afraid.

being patient with me when I was impatient with you.

never failing to give me a kiss when I wanted one.

resisting telling my friends embarrassing stories about me.

Thank you, Dad, for

allowing me to use your favorite toys.

Thank you, Dad, for

accepting there are some things about me
that are different from you.

Thank you, Dad, for . . .

always accepting the affection I wanted to give you.

giving me your affection, even when I didn't seem to want it.

allowing me to grow up, even when you thought
you weren't ready for it.

Thank you, Dad, for

raising me with reason rather than might.

Thank you, Dad, for

being the pillar of strength for our family.

Thank you, Dad, for

encouraging and helping me to pursue my dreams.

Thank you, Dad, for . . .

letting me get to know who you really are.

still letting me hold your hand whenever I want to.

teaching me to share my time as well as my things.

Thank you, Dad, for . . .

starting my college fund as soon as you did.

those braces, even though I hated them at the time.

making sure I knew how to act around strangers.

Thank you, Dad, for

teaching me how to be competitive but fair.

■   ■   ■   ■   ■   ■

Thank you, Dad, for

showing me how to live with a kick in my step
and fire in my heart.

■   ■   ■   ■   ■   ■

Thank you, Dad, for

making sure we spent time together as a family.

Thank you, Dad, for

everything I can think of, for all those things I'm sure
I have forgotten about, and especially
for those things I never knew you did for me.

Paste your picture here and
write your reason
on the opposite page.

Thank you, Dad, for

_____

Acknowledgments

A book about giving thanks to parents would not be complete without also giving thanks to my Heavenly Father. I confess, I sometimes succumb to human nature and think to myself it was my research, talent, and perseverance that resulted in my success as an author. The truth is, however, years ago I was lost and in despair, and I had not an ounce of experience in creative writing. One evening in a prayer I asked for help and then did my best to go forward with hope. Soon certain events began to transpire—like a friend telling me of a successful little book that eventually inspired me to write; my introduction to Janet Lankford-Moran, the photographer who helped me complete my first book; meeting Ron Pitkin, my publisher, who coincidentally, but not known to me until later, was the publisher of the successful little book that got me started in the first place; and then there are all those events in my life that have been the fabric with which my stories about love, faith, forgiveness, and duty are woven. And now my book about thanks, the only one that has closed with a testimonial such as this, is in your hands. Coincidence? Serendipity? Chance? I think not. I once was lost, but now I'm found. Thank you, God.

To Contact the Author

write in care of the publisher:
Cumberland House Publishing
431 Harding Industrial Drive
Nashville, TN 37211

or e-mail the author:
greg.lang@mindspring.com

visit the author's Web site:
gregoryelang.com